Prince Siddhartha

The Story of Buddha

Written by Jonathan Landaw
Illustrated by Janet Brooke

Wisdom Boston

For
Lara Rose, Arwen, Lise & Chana Dorje
Lisa Maria, Anna Sophia & Kevin Lucas
and all children with much love

WISDOM PUBLICATIONS
361 Newbury Street
Boston, Massachusetts 02115
USA

First published in India in 1978 as
The Story of Buddha

This edition first published in 1984

Library of Congress Cataloging-in-Publication Data

Landaw, Jonathan.
    Prince Siddhartha : the story of Buddha / written by Jonathan Landaw ;
illustrated by Janet Brooke.
        p.   cm.
    Summary: Recounts the story of Prince Siddhartha and how he became Buddha,
the Awakened One.
    Engl. ed. of: The story of Buddha, 1978.
    ISBN 0-86171-016-9
    1. Gautama Buddha—Juvenile literature.   [1. Buddha.]
I. Brooke, Janet, ill. II. Landaw, Jonathan. Story of Buddha.
III. Title.
BQ892.L36 1996
294.3'63—dc20   96–11439
[B]   AC

0 86171 016 9

01 00 99 98 97
9 8 7 6 5

Cover Design by L.J. SAWLIT

Set in Garamond 14 on 19 point with Bembo 36 point italic headings
by Characters of Taunton, Somerset.

Printed and bound in Singapore by Eurasia Press (Offset) Pte. Ltd.

Contents

A Fortunate Birth

Many, many years ago, in a small kingdom in the north of India, something was happening that would change the whole world. Queen Maya, wife of the good King Shuddhodana, lay asleep and had a wondrous dream. She dreamt she saw a brilliant white light shining down to her from the sky, and in the rays of this light was a magnificent elephant. It was pure white and had six large tusks. This elephant of light flew closer and closer to the queen and finally melted into her body. Queen Maya awoke, filled with greater happiness than she had ever felt before.

Quickly she went to the King and together they asked the wise men at the court what this strange and wonderful dream might mean. The wise men answered, "O Your Majesties, this dream is a most excellent one! It means that the Queen will give birth to a son, and this prince will someday become a great man. Not only you, but the entire world is fortunate that the Queen will have such a special child." Hearing this good news, the King and Queen were overjoyed. The King was especially happy because he longed for a son who would someday rule

the kingdom in his place. And now it seemed his wish was being granted.

It was the custom in those days for a woman to return to her parents' home in order to give birth. And so, when the time had almost come for the baby to be born, Queen Maya and many of her friends and attendants left the palace of the King and began the journey to her childhood home.

They had not travelled far when the Queen asked that they stop and rest. She knew the baby would be born very soon. They had reached the beautiful gardens of Lumbini and the Queen went into this garden looking for a comfortable place in which she could give birth. The stories say that even the animals and plants, somehow understanding what a special child was about to be born, wanted to help. A large tree bent down one of its branches and the Queen took hold of it with her right hand. Supporting herself in this way, she gave birth to a son. The attendants cradled the baby in their arms and were amazed at how beautiful he was and how peaceful he seemed.

At that moment, throughout the land, there was a great feeling of peace and happiness. People forgot their troubles, ceased their quarrels and felt great love and friendship for one another. Some people saw rainbows suddenly appear in the sky, and many other beautiful and unusual sights were seen.

Wise men from all over the kingdom noticed these signs of peace and joy and excitedly said to each other, "Something very fortunate has just happened. Look at all these wonderful signs! It must certainly be a special day!"

Queen Maya, unaware that her joy at having a son was being shared at that very moment throughout the kingdom, took the new-born baby in her arms and returned to the palace of the King. It was the beginning of the fourth Indian month (May-June) and the moon was growing full.

A Holy Man's Visit

With great rejoicing, King Shuddhodana greeted his Queen and his new son. Splendid festivals were held and the whole kingdom was decked in beautifully coloured banners. It was a time of great happiness and peace. There was so much gladness everywhere that his parents decided to name the Prince "Siddhartha", which means "the one who has brought about all good".

Now the wise men made new predictions about the baby. "O King," they said, "the signs of the Prince's birth are most favourable. Your son will grow up to be even greater than you are now!" This news made the King very proud. "If these wise men are correct," he thought, "my son, Prince Siddhartha, may one day be the ruler not only of my small kingdom, but perhaps of the entire world! What a great honour for me and my family!"

In the first few days after his birth, many people came to the palace to see the new baby. One of these visitors was an old man named Asita. Asita was a hermit who lived by himself in the distant forests, and he was known to be a very holy person. The King and Queen were surprised that Asita would leave his forest home and appear at their court, "We are very honoured that you have come to visit us, O holy teacher," they said with great respect. "Please tell us the purpose of your journey and we shall serve you in any way we can."

Asita answered them, "I thank you for your kind welcome. I have come a great distance to visit you because of the wonderful signs I have recently seen. They tell me that the son recently born to you will gain great spiritual knowledge for the benefit of all people. Since I have spent my entire life trying to gain such holy wisdom, I came here as quickly as possible to see him for myself."

The King was very excited and hurried to where the baby Prince lay sleeping. He carefully picked up his son and brought him back to Asita. For a long time the holy man gazed at the infant, saying nothing. Finally he stepped back, looked sadly up at the sky, sighed heavily and began to cry.

Seeing Asita weep, the King and Queen became very frightened. They were afraid that the holy man had seen something wrong with their child. With tears in his eyes, the King fell to his knees and cried out, "O holy teacher, what have you seen that makes you weep? Didn't you and all the other wise men say that my son was born to be a great man, to gain supreme knowledge? But now, when you look at my baby you cry. Does this mean that the Prince will die soon? Or

will something else very terrible happen to him? He is my only child and I love him dearly. Please tell me quickly what you have seen, for my heart is shaking with sadness and fear."

Then with a very kind look, Asita calmed the new parents and told them not to worry. "Do not be upset," he told them. "I am not crying because of something bad I saw for the Prince. In fact, now that I have seen your son, I know for certain that he will grow up to be more than just a great man. There are special signs that I have seen on this child — such as the light that shines from his fingers — that tell me he will have a glorious future.

"If your son decides to stay with you and become a king, he will be the greatest king in history. He will rule a vast realm and bring his people much peace and happiness. But if he decides *not* to become a king, his future will be even greater! He will become a great teacher, showing all people how to live with peace and love in their hearts. Seeing the sadness in the world he will leave your palace and discover a way to end all suffering. Then he will teach this way to whoever will listen.

"No, dear King and Queen, I was not crying for the child. I was crying for myself. You see, I have spent my whole life looking for the truth, searching for a way to end all suffering. And today I have met the child who will someday teach everything I have wanted to learn. But by the time he is old enough to teach, I shall already have died. Thus, I shall not be able to learn from him in this life. That is why I am so sad. But you, O fortunate parents, should not be sad. Rejoice that you have such a wonderful child."

Then Asita took one long, last look at the child, and slowly left the palace. The King watched him leave and then turned towards his son. He was very happy that there was no danger to the Prince's life. He thought, "Asita has said that Siddhartha will become either a great king or a great teacher. It would be much better if *first* he became a king. How proud I would be to have such a famous and powerful son! Then, when he is old like Asita, he can become a holy man if he wants."

So, thinking like this, King Shuddhodana stood happily with his baby in his arms, dreaming of the fame that his son would someday have.

The Kind Prince

While the new baby was still very young, his mother, Queen Maya, died. Shortly before she passed away, the Queen said to her sister, "Soon I shall not be able to take care of my baby anymore. Dear Sister, after I have gone, please look after Siddhartha for me."

Her sister promised that she would. She loved the little Prince very much and brought him up as if he were her own child.

The Prince grew into a bright, handsome and kind-hearted boy. His father, the King, arranged for him to be educated by the best teachers in the kingdom, and very quickly he showed his remarkable intelligence. After the first few days of classes the teachers reported to the King, "Your Majesty," they said, "the Prince does not need us anymore. After only a few lessons he has learned everything we have to teach him. In fact, he has taught us a few things that we ourselves never knew before!"

Hearing this, the King's pride in his son grew even greater. "With his intelligence, my son will certainly grow up to be a wise and powerful king," he thought, and this made the King very happy.

But there was something else about this boy that was even more remarkable than his intelligence. He had a very kind, gentle and loving nature. The rest of his young playmates enjoyed the rough and tumble games of small children, or pretended they were soldiers and fought with one another. But Prince Siddhartha quietly spent most of his time alone.

He loved the small animals that lived in the palace gardens and became friendly with them all. The animals knew that

"Your Majesty, the Prince has learned everything we have to teach him."

the Prince would never hurt them, so they were not afraid of him. Even the wild animals, who would run away if anyone else came near, came to greet the Prince when he entered the garden. They approached him fearlessly and ate from his hand the food he always brought with him for them.

One day as the Prince was sitting in the garden, a flock of white swans flew overhead. Suddenly an arrow shot up into the air, striking one of them. It fell out of the sky and landed at the Prince's feet, the arrow still stuck into its wing.

"Oh, you poor swan," Siddhartha whispered as he gently picked up the wounded bird, "do not be afraid. I shall take care of you. Here, let me remove this arrow." Then, with one hand he gently stroked the bird, calming its fear. With his other hand he slowly pulled out the painful arrow. The Prince was carrying a special lotion with him and softly rubbed it into the bird's wing, all the time speaking in a low, pleasant voice so that the swan would not become afraid. Finally he took off his own silk shirt and wrapped it around the bird to keep it warm.

After a short time, another young boy came running into the garden. It was the Prince's cousin, Devadatta. He was carrying a bow and some arrows and he was very excited.

"Siddhartha, Siddhartha," he shouted, "great news! I got a swan! You should have seen me; I hit it with my first shot! It fell down somewhere near here. Help me look for it."

Then Devadatta noticed one of his arrows, with blood still on its tip, lying on the ground near Siddhartha's feet. Looking closer he saw that the Prince was holding something in his arms, and realized it was the swan he was searching for. "Hey, you took my swan," he yelled. "Give it back to me. I shot it and it's mine!" Devadatta grabbed at the bird, but the Prince held onto it, keeping his angry cousin from even touching the injured creature.

"I found this bird lying here bleeding," the Prince said firmly, "and I don't plan to give it to anyone while it is still wounded."

"But it's mine!" shouted Devadatta again. "I shot it fair and square, and you've stolen it from me. Give it back or I'll *take* it back."

The two boys stood arguing like this for some time. Devadatta was getting angrier and angrier, but Siddhartha refused to give him the swan. Finally, the Prince said, "When two grown-ups have a quarrel like this, they settle it in court. In front of a group of wise people, each one explains the story of what happened. Then the wise people decide who is right. I think you and I should do the same."

Devadatta did not like this idea very much, but because it was the only way he could ever get the swan back, he agreed. So the two of them went to the palace and appeared in front of the King and his ministers. The people at court smiled at each other when they heard what these two children wanted. "To think," they said, "that they want to take up our time over a mere bird!" But the King said, "Both Siddhartha and Devadatta are royal princes, and I am glad they brought their quarrel to us. I think it is very important that, as future rulers, they become used to the ways of this court. Let the trial begin!"

So in turn each of the boys described what happened. Then the ministers tried to decide which boy was right and should therefore have the swan. Some thought, "Devadatta shot the bird; therefore it should belong to him." Others thought, "Siddhartha found the swan; therefore it should belong to him." And for a long time the ministers talked and argued about the case.

Finally, into the court came a very old man whom no one remembered ever seeing before. But because he looked so wise, they told him the story of the boys and their swan. After listening to what they had to say, he declared, "Everyone values his or her life more than anything else in the world. Therefore, I think that the swan belongs to the

24

person who tried to *save* its life, not to the person who tried to take its life away. Give the swan to Siddhartha."

Everyone agreed that what the wise man said was true, so they decided to let the Prince keep the swan. Later, when the King tried to find the old man and reward him for his wisdom, he was nowhere to be found. "This is very strange," the King thought. "I wonder where he came from and where he went." But no one knew. This was just one of the many unusual things that happened concerning the Prince, so many people thought he must be a very special child indeed!

The Marriage Contest

As the Prince grew older, his kindness made him well-loved by everyone who knew him. But his father was worried. "Siddhartha is too gentle and sensitive," he thought. "I want him to grow up to be a great king and kings must be strong and powerful. But the Prince is more interested in sitting by himself in the garden than he is in learning how to be the ruler of a kingdom. I am afraid that my son will soon want to leave the palace and follow the lonely life of holy men like Asita. If he does this he will never become a great king."

These thoughts bothered the King very much. He sent for his most trusted ministers and asked them what he could do. Finally one of them suggested, "O King, your son sits and dreams of *other* worlds only because he is not yet attached to anything in *this* world. Find him a wife, let him get married and have children, and soon he will stop dreaming and become interested in learning how to rule the kingdom."

The King thought this was an excellent idea. So he arranged for a large banquet at the palace. All the young women from

The King was worried.

noble families were invited. At the end of the evening the Prince was asked to give presents to each of the guests, while several ministers watched him closely to see which of the young women the Prince seemed to like.

The women, who were scarcely more than young girls, were all very embarrassed to appear before the Prince. He looked so handsome but so distant as he stood in front of the table bearing all the expensive gifts. One by one they shyly went up to him, timidly looking downwards as they approached. They silently accepted the jewel or bracelet or other gift, and quickly returned to their places.

Finally, only one young woman was left. She was Yasodhara, the daughter of a neighbouring king. Unlike the others, she approached the Prince without any shyness. For the first time that evening, the young Prince looked directly at the woman before him. She was very beautiful and the Prince was immediately attracted to her.

They stood in silence for a while, looking into each other's eyes. Then Yasodhara spoke, "O Prince, where is the gift for me?" The Prince was startled, as if awakening from a dream. He looked down at the table and saw it was empty. All the gifts had already been given out to the other guests.

"Here, take this," said the Prince, removing his own ring from his finger. "This is for you." Yasodhara graciously accepted the ring and walked slowly back to her place.

The ministers saw all that happened and excitedly ran to the King. "Sire!" they reported happily, "we have found the perfect bride for the Prince. She is Princess Yasodhara, daughter of your neighbour, King Suprabuddha. Let us immediately go to this King and arrange for the marrriage of his daughter and your son."

King Shuddhodana agreed and soon afterwards visited Yasodhara's father. The other king greeted him warmly and said, "I am sure that your son is a fine young man, but I cannot give my daughter away to just anyone. Many other princes want to marry her, and they are all excellent young men. They are skilled in riding, archery and other royal sports. Therefore, if your son wants to marry my daughter, he will have to compete in a contest with the other suitors, as is our custom."

And so it was arranged for a great contest to be held, with beautiful Yasodhara as the prize. King Shuddhodana was worried. He thought, "My son has never showed the slightest interest in warrior games. How can he ever win this contest?" But the Prince understood his father's fears and said to him, "Do not be worried. I am prepared to do whatever is necessary to win Yasodhara as my bride."

The first event was archery. The other men placed their targets a long distance away, yet each was able to hit the bull's-eye. And when it was Devadatta's turn — for Siddhartha's cousin was also one of the suitors — he not only hit the bull's-eye, but sent his arrow right through the target until it stuck out the other side. The crowd cheered, but Yasodhara covered her eyes in fright. "How can my beloved Siddhartha ever beat that shot?" she thought. "How dreadful if I had to marry Devadatta!"

But the Prince was confident. When it was his turn he had his target placed so far away that most of the people could hardly even see it. Then he took an arrow from his quiver and pulled back on his bow. The Prince was so strong, however, that the bow burst in half; he had drawn it back so far!

"Please fetch me another bow," the Prince asked, "but a much stronger one this time so it will not break like the other one." Then a minister called out, "O Prince, there is a very old bow in the palace. It belonged to one of the greatest warriors of the past. But since he died many years ago no one has been strong enough to string it, much less shoot it."

"I shall use that one," said the Prince, and everyone was amazed. When he was handed the bow he carefully bent it and strung it easily. Then he notched an arrow on the string, drew it back so far that the ends of the bow almost touched, aimed,

and let the arrow fly. Twang! The bow made such a loud sound that people in far away villages heard it. The arrow shot away so fast that when it hit the distant target — right in the centre of the bull's-eye — it did not even slow down, but continued to fly until it was out of sight.

The crowd roared in delight! "The Prince has won! The Prince has won!" But archery was only the first event of the day; the next contest was in swordsmanship.

Each young man selected a tree and showed his strength by slashing through it with his sword. One suitor cut through a tree six inches thick, another nine inches, and a third cut through a tree a foot thick with a single stroke of his sword!

Then it was the Prince's turn. He selected a tree that had two trunks growing side by side. He swung his sword so quickly that it cut through the tree faster than anyone could see. His sword was so sharp and his cut so even that the tree did not even fall over. Instead it remained standing, perfectly balanced. When they saw the tree still standing upright, the crowd and especially Yasodhara moaned, "He has failed. The Prince's sword did not even cut into the first trunk."

But just then a breeze stirred up and blew over the neatly severed tree trunks. The crowd's moans turned into cheers, and again they shouted, "The Prince has won!"

The final contest was in horsemanship. A wild horse, which had never been ridden before, was held down by several strong men while each young suitor tried to mount it. But the horse bucked and kicked so furiously that none of them could stay on its back for more than a few seconds. Finally one young man managed to hold on and the attendants let go of the horse. But it jumped and lunged about with such fury and anger that the rider was thrown to the ground. And he would have been trampled if the men had not rushed out and pulled him to safety.

The crowd began screaming loudly, "Stop the contest! Don't let the Prince near that horse! It is too dangerous; the horse will kill him!" But Siddhartha had no fear. "Gentleness can be more powerful than brute strength," he thought, and slowly reached out and took hold of a small tuft of hair that grew from the horse's forehead. Speaking in a low and pleasant voice, and gently stroking the wild horse's head and sides, he calmed its anger, rage and fear.

Soon the horse was so gentle that it began licking Siddhartha's hand. Then, still whispering sweetly to the horse, the Prince climbed onto its back. While the crowd roared happily, he paraded the steed in front of the kings and ministers, and bowed low to his fair prize, the lovely Yasodhara. The contest was over; young Siddhartha had won! And he had done so not only by his great strength, but by his gentleness and kindness as well.

The Pleasure Palaces

Soon afterwards, Prince Siddhartha and Princess Yasodhara were married. The King wanted to be certain that his son would never desire to leave the kingdom, so he ordered not one but three magnificent palaces to be built for the new couple. "Make them as beautiful as possible," he told the chief builder. "I want them to be so magnificent that the people entering them will think they are in heaven.

"I want one to be a summer palace, made of cool marble and surrounded by refreshing pools and fountains. The second will be the winter palace, warm and comfortable. And the third will be for the rainy season. Place these palaces in the middle of a large park, with beautiful scenery in every direction. And surround the park with a large wall, so that nothing unpleasant from the outside world can ever get in. Everything is to be so perfect that Prince Siddhartha will never be tempted to leave."

The King did everything possible to make these new homes attractive to the Prince. He had the most skilled musicians in his kingdom play there throughout the day and into the night. All the servants were beautiful young dancing girls, and the chefs in the kitchen were instructed to serve a never-ending variety of delicious food. Nothing was allowed into the palaces that might disturb the Prince's mind and make him want to leave.

And so for many years Prince Siddhartha lived in these heavenly surroundings. From morning to night he was entertained in a thousand ways. He never heard any sound that was not sweet and pleasant and never saw anything that was not beautiful. For instance, if one of the servant girls became ill, she was removed from the palace and was not allowed to return until she was better again.

In this way the Prince never saw sickness or anything that might disturb his gentle mind. The King ordered that no one speaking to the Prince should ever mention anything sad or depressing. And even if one of the plants in the garden began to droop or wilt, it was immediately snipped off by a special gardener. Thus the Prince never even saw a faded or dying flower! In all these ways, then, he was kept ignorant of the suffering and unpleasantness in the world.

Time passed as if in a dream. Yasodhara gave birth to a son, Rahula, and everything seemed perfect. The King was very pleased, glad that his plan to keep the Prince interested in the royal life was working out so well. But it was not meant that Siddhartha, whose birth was the cause for all the world's rejoicing, should pass his life in such idle splendour. Eventually, when the time was right, he would discover the true purpose of his life.

A Song of Beauty

One evening after dinner, Prince Siddhartha lay reclining on his couch, his head resting in Yasodhara's lap. The musicians were playing sweet melodies and the servant girls were whispering and laughing quietly to each other. The evening was like so many the Prince had known since moving into the pleasure palaces. But this night he felt restless. Turning to one of his favourite singers, he requested, "Please lull us to sleep with a song. Choose a tune you have never sung for me before."

The singer graciously agreed and began to make up a new song from the words that floated through her mind, all the while accompanying herself on a stringed instrument. She sang of the beauties of the world, of the distant lands where she had travelled as a child, of golden cities where happy people lived.

The song enchanted the Prince and when it was over he asked the singer, "Tell me truly, are there really such beautiful places beyond these garden walls? What kind of lives do the people in the city live? Are there things in this world more lovely than what I have seen in these magnificent palaces? Please, tell me all you know."

"O Prince," she answered, "surely these palaces of yours are the most magnificent, but there are many other beautiful things to be seen in this wide world. There are cities and towns, mountains and valleys, distant lands where people speak strange languages. There are many things that I have seen, and many more that I have only heard about. Your palaces and gardens are indeed beautiful, but there is much to see outside their walls."

Hearing this, the Prince became interested in seeing all these strange wonderful things for himself. For so many years he had been content to live within the pleasure palaces and gardens, completely forgetting about the world beyond. It was as if he had been living in a dream for all those years and now he was beginning to wake up. He was no longer satisfied to remain within the beautiful surroundings he knew so well; instead, he desired to journey forth and see what other wonders the world had in store for him. So he sent a message to the King requesting him to arrange a travel party into the city beyond the garden walls.

The King received his son's message and thought to himself, "So now my son wishes to see our kingdom. So be it! He has stayed long enough inside his pleasure palaces. It is time for him to see the kingdom he will someday rule."

An Unexpected Sight

The King still wanted to be certain that his son would not see anything on his trip that might disturb his mind. This might make him want to leave the kingdom and follow the holy life. So the day before the Prince was about to travel to the city, the King sent his servants and soldiers out with the message: "By order of the King! Tomorrow the royal Prince Siddhartha will visit the capital city of Kapilavastu. Decorate your houses and streets and let everything be colourful in his honour. Let those who are sick or old or in any way unhealthy stay indoors tomorrow.

Nothing should be seen in the city that is not young and fair and beautiful." And then, very gently, the soldiers took all the street beggars and brought them to a part of the city where the Prince would not visit.

When morning came, the charioteer Channa groomed the Prince's favourite horse, Kantaka, and drove out through the palace gates with his royal passenger.

It was the first time the Prince had seen Kapilavastu since he was a small child, and it was the first time that most of the citizens of the city had ever seen their Prince. Everyone was excited and lined the newly decorated streets to catch a glimpse of the handsome young man as he rode by. "How tall and good-looking he is!" they said to one another. "How bright his eyes and noble his brow! We are indeed fortunate that someday he will be our king."

And the Prince, too, was delighted. The city was sparkling and clean and everywhere he saw people laughing and cheering and even dancing. The streets where he rode were covered with the flower petals the citizens joyously threw their beloved Prince. "The song was true," he remembered happily. "This is indeed a golden, beautiful and wondrous city!"

But as the Prince and his charioteer were riding by they spotted a bent, sad-looking person among the joyous crowd. Curious — for the Prince had never seen anything like this before — he turned and asked, "Channa who is that person over there? Why is he stooping over and not dancing like the others? Why is his face not smooth and shining like everyone else's; why is it pale and wrinkled? Why is he so different from the others?"

And Channa pointed to that man, who remained unseen by everyone else, and answered the Prince, "Why Sir, that is just an old man."

"Old?" the Prince questioned. "Was this man always 'old' like this before, or did it happen to him recently?"

"Neither, O Prince," Channa answered. "Many years ago that wrinkled man before you was as young and strong as all the others you see here today. But slowly he lost his strength. His body became bent, the colour faded from his cheeks, he lost most of his teeth, and now he appears the way he does."

Surprised and saddened, Siddhartha asked again, "That poor man, is he the only one suffering the weaknesses of old age? Or are there any others like him?"

"Surely you know, O Prince, that everyone must experience old age. You, me, your wife Yasodhara, Rahula, everyone at the palace — we are all growing older every moment. Someday most of us will look like that man.

These words so shocked the gentle Prince that for a long time he remained speechless. He looked like a person who had just been frightened by a sudden lightning flash. Finally he regained his voice and spoke, "O Channa, I have seen something today that I never expected to see. In the midst of all these happy young people this vision of old age frightens me.

Turn the chariot back to the palace; all the enjoyment of this trip has fled. Turn back; I wish to see no more."

Channa did as commanded. When they arrived back home, the Prince entered his palace without greeting anyone, hurried upstairs to his own room, and sat by himself for a long time. Everyone noticed how strangely he acted and tried hard to cheer him up. But nothing helped. At dinner he did not touch any of his food, even though the chef had prepared his favourite meal. He paid no attention to the music and dancing, but sat by himself thinking, "Old age, old age, old age...."

The Second Journey

The King heard about his son's unhappy mood and wondered what could have gone wrong. "He needs more variety," the King thought. "I'll plan another trip for him, but this time to an even more beautiful part of the city."

And so Channa prepared Kantaka again, and again they rode out into Kapilavastu. The streets were decorated as before, and the people were again happy to see their Prince. But this time, seen only by Siddhartha and his charioteer, a vision of a sick person appeared in the crowd of laughing people.

"Look Channa," the Prince called out. "Who is that man who coughs so violently, who shakes his body and cries so pitifully?"

"That is a sick person, O Prince."

"Why is he 'sick'?" he asked.

"People become sick for many reasons, Sire. Perhaps he ate some bad food or let himself become too cold. Now his body is out of balance and he feels feverish."

"Do even happy people like those in the crowd ever become sick?"

"Oh yes," answered the charioteer. "A person might be healthy one day and sick the next. No one is safe from illness."

For the second time the Prince was deeply shocked. I cannot understand," he said, "how people can be so carefree and happy knowing that sickness might strike them at any time. Please, turn back the chariot. I have seen more than enough for one day."

When he returned to the palace, the Prince was even more unhappy than before. Nothing anyone did could make him smile, and he did not want to speak to anyone. When the King found out about his son's unhappiness he became very worried and confused. "I have tried everything to make my son happy, but lately his heart is filled with gloom. I must ask my ministers what I can do to brighten my son's spirits."

They suggested that the next time the Prince wanted to leave the palace grounds, he should not go alone. Rather, he should be accompanied by singers, dancers and nobles from the court. And they should plan to visit a specially prepared garden where the Prince could be amused and distracted by all sorts of entertainment.

And so, when Prince Siddhartha again requested to visit the city beyond the garden walls, many arrangements were made to make the journey as enjoyable as possible. The city was beautified even more than before. All unpleasant sights were removed and a special park was prepared with all manner of delights.

The Final Shock

Siddhartha and Channa again left the palace by chariot. And for a third time a vision appeared that only the Prince and his charioteer could see. A group of sad-eyed people, carrying a long box in which a body covered in a white sheet lay, appeared from one of the houses and slowly made its way down one of the side streets.

"Channa, why is that man in the box lying so still? Is he asleep? And why are all those people crying? Where are they taking him?"

"He is a dead man, Sire. They are going to the river where they will burn his body."

The Prince was confused. "What do you mean by 'dead'? And if they burn his body, will it not hurt him? Please, Channa, explain what you mean so I can understand."

And so Channa explained, telling the Prince the truths his father had tried to hide from him all these years. "That man was once alive, as you and I are now. He was born, grew into a child, then he became a young man. He experienced the many pleasures and pains of life, raised a family, worked for a living and grew older. Then he began to get weaker and weaker. He was confined to his bed. Soon he was unable to recognize even his closest friends. He grew worse and eventually his breath left his body. In this way his understanding and life-force came to an end. Now he is dead. All that is left behind to see is the body he cared for so much while he was still alive. It lies there cold and without feeling. When his family burns the body he will not feel anything, because he has already left it behind."

"Tell me, Channa, is it unusual for people to die like this?" The charioteer answered, "No, my Prince, not at all. It is true that there are *some* people who never get the chance to grow old, and there are *some* who are very rarely sick. But *everyone*, without exception, must one day die."

These words, uttered innocently by the charioteer, shocked the Prince deeply. "Do you mean," he exclaimed passionately, "that one day my wife, my child, my friends and myself will all

56

be dead? And all these people I see here today, all dressed up and so radiant, will also die? Oh, how blind the world is that it can dance and sing while death is just waiting for everyone! Why do they all bother to dress themselves in such fine clothes if one day they shall be wearing nothing more than a simple white sheet? Do people have such short memories that they forget about death? Or are their hearts so strong that the thought of death does not bother them? Come, Channa, turn the chariot around. I wish to return to the palace and think."

But instead, Channa drove the chariot to a beautiful garden. There all the most charming singers and dancers from the palace were waiting, along with the musicians, ministers and a large feast prepared by the palace chefs. They all welcomed the Prince joyfully and cheered when he stepped from the chariot. But the Prince did not smile, nor did he say anything. His thoughts were totally absorbed in what he had seen that day.

Fading Pleasures

Everyone tried his or her best to amuse the Prince. The dancing girls flirted with him, hoping to win at least a smile from his handsome but saddened face. Yet Siddhartha did not even seem to notice them. He could not get the visions of old age, sickness and death out of his mind.

One of the ministers, seeing that the Prince was not enjoying any of the splendid arrangements that had been made for him, came over to the Prince. In the joking manner of a friend he said, "Siddhartha, it is not right that you ignore these lovely dancers and refuse to join the festivities. Come on! You are young and healthy; you should be enjoying yourself. What is the matter? Aren't these women pretty enough for you?"

But the Prince answered him in a voice as strong and low as thunder. "You have misunderstood me. I do not dislike the lovely people and things I see here. But when I think of how quickly their beauty will disappear, how everything changes so fast, I cannot find much pleasure in them anymore.

"If there were no old age, sickness and death, then I, too, could find great pleasure in such lovely objects. But in the middle of such unhappiness, knowing what awaits us all in the future, how can I be satisfied with pleasures that will fade so quickly?

"You, my friend, must have a stronger heart than mine if you can be amused so easily. But for me, everything I see is on fire with suffering. Until I find a way out of this suffering, such worldly amusements do not interest me at all."

And so, unable to brighten the Prince's mood, everyone returned sadly to the palace. When the ministers told the King that his son could not be entertained or distracted by anything, he felt so much grief that he could not sleep. "O, my beloved son," he thought to himself, "what else can I do to keep you here in my kingdom with me? What other pleasures can I provide so that you will stay?" And with such worried thoughts, fearful that he would soon lose his only son, the King spent the night in despair.

A Vision of Peace

The Prince sank deeper and deeper into gloom. He seemed to lose interest in everything. He hardly ate anything anymore, and as a result began to look pale and unhealthy. The King and everyone else were very upset that these unhappy changes had come over their beloved Siddhartha.

One day he appeared before the King. "Father," he began, "lately my mind has been very troubled. I feel restless and would like your permission to leave the palace once again. Perhaps a change of scenery will do me good."

The King was quick to agree to his son's request, for he would do anything to please him and make him happy again. But, as before, he asked some of his most trusted ministers to stay close to the Prince and keep an eye on him.

This time Siddhartha saddled Kantaka himself and rode out of the palace grounds in search of some beautiful countryside. Finally he came to the edge of some farmland and dismounted. The ministers followed close behind. They tried to gain his attention with stories, news and gossip of the court. But the

Prince had no interest in such idle talk, and soon the ministers left him alone and walked away, still chattering amongst themselves.

Siddhartha looked out over the farmland. A man and his oxen were ploughing the field, the birds were singing and the sun was shining brightly. "It is so beautiful here," he thought. "The ploughed rows in the field look like ripples on a lake."

He sat down, and his mind relaxed for the first time in a long while. But as he looked closer at the scene before him, he began to notice things he had not seen before.

Where the plough had come by and cut rows into the soil, he saw the bodies of hundreds of small insects that had been killed by its blade. He saw hundreds more running back and forth in confusion now that their homes had been destroyed.

He also noticed that the birds were not just gaily singing. They were constantly searching for food, swooping down to snatch up the frightened insects. And the smaller birds darted about in fear, scared of the hawks and other large birds who circled hungrily above them.

He noticed that the oxen laboured heavily while trying to drag the heavy plough through the ground. The lashes of the farmer's whip cut painful blisters into their sweating sides.

And the farmer, too, worked hard. Like the beasts, his rough and sunburnt body glistened with sweat.

"Such a circle of misery," thought the Prince. "This farmer, his animals, the birds and the insects — they work all day trying to be happy and comfortable, to have enough to eat. But, in fact, they are constantly killing and hurting each other, and themselves! How pitiful the world seems to me."

The Prince's heart was filled with compassion for all these suffering creatures. He hated to see them so unhappy.

He found a shady place to sit under a rose-apple tree and began to meditate deeply on what he had seen. As he looked deeper and deeper in the nature of the suffering he had seen, his mind became more and more concentrated and calm. He experienced a quietness unlike anything he had ever known before.

With his mind now at rest he began to think, "Every living thing is searching for happiness. Yet most are so blinded by their ignorance and desires that they find nothing but misery. Fear, disappointment, hunger, old age, sickness, death — these are the rewards they find for all their trouble!"

"Now that I have seen this, I have no more interest in the small and changeable pleasures of this world. I must find

something that will bring me *lasting* peace and happiness. But how can I be content to free only myself from suffering? I must figure out a way to help all other living creatures as well. They have been so kind to me, and they are suffering so much! I must search for a way to end all this suffering and then share it with everyone else."

When Prince Siddhartha had finished this compassionate meditation he opened his eyes. Standing before him, dressed like a poor beggar, was a man he had never seen before. His eyes were calm and bright and he had the look of great peace on his face.

"Please tell me," the Prince asked, "who are you?"

The man answered, "I am someone who has become frightened by the sufferings of the world. I have grown tired of the so-called pleasures to be found in the company of others, so now I wander about alone. I have given up my home and now live and sleep in caves, in the forest or wherever I find myself. My only interest is in finding the highest and most perfect happiness." When he had spoken these words, the man disappeared as if by magic, leaving the Prince both astonished and overjoyed.

"At last I have found the true purpose of my life," Siddhartha thought. "I, too, shall give up my home and begin my search for true happiness and the end of all suffering!"

And so, with a firm mind and a steady heart, he mounted his horse Kantaka and rode back to the palace.

A Father's Fear

Upon his arrival home the Prince immediately went to the King's room. Pressing his hands together, as was the custom when making an important request, he announced, "I wish to become a homeless wanderer and search for the end of all suffering. Grant me your permission, Father, to leave the palace."

From the time his son was a baby, the King had feared that someday he would have to hear this dreaded request. But still his son's words came as a great shock to him. In a voice choked with tears, he replied, "Dearest Son, forget this idea of leaving. You are still much too young to follow the lonely life of a holy man. Wait until you are older. Meanwhile stay here in Kapilavastu and rule my kingdom."

"O Father, I shall stay here only if you can promise me four things. Tell me that I shall never grow old, that I shall never become ill, that I shall never die and that I shall never be unhappy. If you cannot promise me these things, then I must leave immediately."

The King was shocked by these strange words and began to get angry. "Forget these foolish ideas, Siddhartha," he said loudly.

But the Prince remained firm. "Father, if you cannot save me from the sufferings of old age, sickness, death and unhappiness, then you must let me go and try to save myself. It is not right to keep me a prisoner here."

But the King would hear no more. "Do not let the Prince leave! Set a guard around the palace grounds!" he shouted to his ministers and then angrily stormed out of the room.

Escape

Siddhartha left the King's room and returned to his palace. He passed through the beautifully decorated rooms, the magnificent hallways, past the sparkling fountains and into his rooms on the upper storey. He walked among the talented musicians and past the beautiful serving girls. But none of these delights affected his mind. He had only one thought, and that was to leave.

That night after dinner a strange force seemed to enter the palace. One by one the musicians and dancers and servants became drowsy and fell asleep. Finally even Yasodhara fell asleep next to her baby Rahula. Only Siddhartha remained awake. Now that he knew what he must do with his life, he would never again allow himself to fall under the spell of worldly comforts and distractions. Others might be content to sleep and dream, but he had more important work to do, and for that he had to be fully awake.

Now was the perfect chance for the Prince to escape. But before he left he thought to himself, "I would like to hold my son in my arms before I depart; since he was born I have barely had the chance to touch him." Yet when he saw his wife and child lying together he realized that there was no way for him to pick Rahula up without rousing Yasodhara. "If she wakes up," he thought, "it will be very difficult for me to leave. No, if I am to do what I must do, I should leave quickly and quietly while everyone is asleep."

Stepping carefully around the sleeping bodies, he reached the window and climbed out onto the roof and then down to the ground. He went to where Channa, the charioteer, was sleeping and gently woke him up. "Hurry, Channa, saddle my horse. I wish to ride tonight."

Channa was surprised that the Prince would want to go out in the middle of the night, but he did as he was asked. He saddled Kantaka and led him to the Prince. Siddhartha patted his horse and whispered, "Kantaka, my old friend, we must be very quiet. I don't want to wake up any of the guards. Tonight is a very special night."

As the three of them approached the heavy gates at the edge of the gardens, the doors suddenly opened by themselves. Silently they rode out into the night. When they reached the edge of the city, the Prince looked back and vowed to himself, "Until I learn how to conquer all sufferings, I shall not return to this fair city of Kapilavastu!"

They rode all night. Just as the morning sun was about to rise they reached a quiet forest where many holy people lived.

The Prince was happy and thought to himself, "Now my real journey has begun." Then he turned to Channa and said, "My friend, I thank you deeply for your help. I have reached the place I wanted. Now it is time for you to take my horse and return to the palace."

Channa could not believe that the Prince would not be returning to the palace with him. He stood there confused, tears beginning to fill his eyes. The Prince understood his grief and spoke to him again very softly. "My faithful Channa, do not cry. Sooner or later we all have to say goodbye. Here, take these royal jewels I am wearing; I shall not need them anymore. Return to the palace and tell my father that I have not left in anger. It is not that I do not love my family anymore. Rather, it is because I love them all so much that I must leave them for now. If I fail, then it really makes little difference that I am leaving this day. Sooner or later death would pull us apart anyway. Go now, and let me begin my search."

Channa realised that there was no way he could change the Prince's mind. He took Kantaka's reins from the Prince and slowly led the horse away. Many times both the charioteer and Kantaka looked back at the Prince with tears in their eyes. Eventually they reached Kapilavastu where Channa had the sad duty of telling everyone that Siddhartha had left the royal life forever.

The Journey Begins

As Siddhartha stood alone in the forest, ready to begin his great adventure, he thought, "From today onwards I am no longer a prince. Therefore, it is not right that I continue to look and dress like one." He took his knife and cut off his long, flowing hair, a sign of royalty. Then he met a poor hunter and said to him, "Sir, I have no more need of these silk clothes. If I am to live in the forest I should wear something rough like yours. Let us exchange clothing." The hunter was surprised and delighted to receive such expensive garments in exchange for his own and quickly agreed to Siddhartha's suggestion.

Now that he was properly dressed as a poor seeker of the truth, Siddhartha began to look for a teacher who could show him the way to end all suffering. He wandered through the forests and spoke to all the many holy men he found there. Everywhere he went he was welcomed with respect. Even though he now wore ragged clothes and ate only the poor food he could beg, he was still a very handsome and striking-looking man. When the people in the forest saw him coming they said to each other, "Here comes a very special person.

His face is so strong and determined! If such a man is looking for the truth, he is sure to find it."

Siddhartha studied with several teachers, but was not satisfied with what he learned from them. "What they teach is helpful," he thought, "but it does not lead to perfect happiness." Finally he heard that some very wise men lived in the kingdom of Magadha where King Bimbisara ruled. So he decided to travel far to the south and east to find them.

One day, as he was walking through Rajagriha, the capital city of Magadha, he passed near the palace gates. One of King Bimbisara's ministers saw him and immediately ran to the King.

"Sire," he said excitedly, "I have just seen a most unusual man in the city. He is dressed in rags and begs his food from door to door, but I am sure he must be a great person. His face is so strong and he walks with such dignity. It almost seems that a special light shines from him!"

The King was very interested and asked that Siddhartha be brought before him. They talked together for a while and the King was very impressed by his intelligence, modesty and kind manner. Then the King said, "I have never met a man I felt I could trust more than you. Please settle here in Rajagriha and help me rule my kingdom."

But Siddhartha replied politely, "O King, I have already had the chance to rule a kingdom, but I had to refuse. I am not

interested in wealth or power, only in the path of truth. I thank
you for your offer, but I have come to your kingdom only to
find teachers who can help me with my search."

Then the King bowed to the man in rags and said, "I wish
you luck in your journey. If you do find what you are looking
for, please return here and teach it to me. But even if you fail,
you are always welcome to return to my palace." Siddhartha
thanked him very much and continued on his way.

81

Six Years of Struggle

Eventually Siddhartha came to the forest where the wise men lived. He studied first with Arada and then with Udraka. In a short time he mastered everything they had to teach. But still he was not satisfied. "My teachers are holy people, but what they have taught me does not bring an end to all suffering. I must continue to search on my own."

He continued his travels until he came to the Nairangana River, near the holy town of Gaya. He crossed the river and entered the forests on the other side. There he found a group of five men. Their life was extremely simple. They ate very little food, lived out in the open, and sat perfectly still for many hours each day.

"Why are you doing such painful things to your bodies?" the Prince asked these men.

"Most people in the world treat their bodies very gently," they answered, "yet still experience much suffering. We feel that if we can learn to master pain, we shall have found the way to control all sufferings."

Siddhartha thought to himself, "For so many years I lived in those luxurious pleasure palaces. I was treated very gently, yet still my mind did not find peace. Perhaps these men are right. I shall join them in their practices and see if this leads to the end of suffering."

And so he began these difficult and painful practices. He sat for hours and hours in the same spot. Even though his legs and back hurt very much, he would not move a muscle. He let himself be burned by the blazing summer sun and chilled by the winter winds. He ate barely enough food to remain alive. But no matter how difficult it was, he thought, "I must continue and discover the way out of all misery!"

The five men were amazed at Siddhartha. They said to themselves, "Never have we seen anyone with as much determination as this man. He drives himself on and on and never quits. If anyone is ever going to succeed in these practices it will be Siddhartha. Let us stay near him so that when he discovers the true path we shall be able to learn it from him."

Siddhartha treated his body more and more harshly. In the beginning he slept only a few hours each night, but eventually he stopped going to sleep altogether! He stopped taking even the one poor meal a day that he used to allow himself, and would eat only the few seeds and berries that the wind blew into his lap.

He grew thinner and thinner. His body lost its radiance and became covered with dust and dirt. He became little more than a living skeleton. But still he did not give up his practices.

Six long years passed. Siddhartha was twenty-nine years old when he left his palaces and all their pleasures behind. Now he was thirty-five, having spend six years with hardly any food, sleep, shelter or decent clothing.

One day he thought to himself, "Am I closer to my goal now than I was six years ago? Or am I still as ignorant as before? When I was a prince and lived in luxury, I had everything a person could desire. I wasted many years in those prisons of pleasure.

"Then I left and began my search. I have lived in forests and caves and have had nothing but poor food and much pain. But I still have not learned how to put an end to suffering. I can see now that it is a mistake to punish my body like this, just as it was a mistake to have wasted so much time in those palaces. To find the truth I must follow a middle path between too much pleasure and too much pain."

He remembered that many years ago, after he had seen the dead man, he had meditated under a rose-apple tree. "After that meditation," he thought, "my mind was very calm and still. I was able to see things clearly for the first time. I shall try to meditate like that again now."

But when he looked at himself he realized, "I have been sitting here for such a long time with no food that I am tired, dirty and weak. I am so thin that I can see my bones through my skin. How can I meditate when I am too hungry and dirty even to think clearly?"

And so he slowly pulled himself up and went to bathe himself in the river. He was so weak, however, that he fell and was almost drowned. With great effort he just managed to pull himself to the shore. Then he sat for a while, resting.

An Offering

In a small village at the edge of the forest lived a herdsman and his wife Sujata. She had just given birth to her first child and was very happy. She took the finest milk from her husband's cows and prepared a delicious meal from it. Now she was taking this food into the forest as an offering to the spirits she thought lived there. She had often prayed to these spirits and wanted to thank them for helping her have such a healthy baby.

As she entered the forest she saw Siddhartha sitting there. His body was thin and weak, but his face was radiant and handsome. Sujata gazed at him in surprise. "I have never seen anyone like that before," she thought to herself. "Perhaps it is the King of the tree spirits himself!" And so she took the specially prepared food and placed it before him.

Siddhartha slowly opened his eyes and saw the bowl in front of him. Smiling silently to Sujata he lifted it to his lips and began to drink. To her amazement, his body grew more and more radiant as he drank. When he was finished he placed the bowl down and thanked her saying, "You thought I was a spirit, but I am only a man in search of the truth. Your offering

has made me strong again. Now I am sure that I shall find the truth. Much good will come from what you have done today. Thank you."

The five men who were living in the forest with Siddhartha saw him accept this special food from Sujata. They were very disappointed and said to themselves, "Siddhartha has given up his search. He is no longer following the holy life. Look, he bathes himself and takes rich food again. How can we stay with such a man any longer? Come. Let us leave this forest and travel to Varanasi. We can continue our practices in the Deer Park near there."

And so they left, thinking that Siddhartha was no longer interested in discovering the truth. But Siddhartha, strengthened by his meal and prepared to meditate, was now ready to find what he had been looking for all these many years. He stood up, waded across the river and headed towards what would be known in later years as the Tree of Enlightenment.

The Great Battle

The moment that the world had been waiting for was now at hand. Siddhartha, who had given up a kingdom in search of truth, was approaching the tree. On his way he passed a man carrying freshly cut grass and asked him for a small bundle. This he would use as his seat.

As he drew closer the air became very still. It was as if the whole world were holding its breath, anxiously awaiting what would happen next. The branches of the tree bent down as if welcoming him to come and sit down under its shade.

Siddhartha carefully arranged the grass into a small cushion and sat down, facing the east. He crossed his legs in a firm meditation posture and rested his hands in his lap. Then he made a bold and determined vow: "I shall not arise from this position until I have reached my goal, even if I die sitting here!" And all the spirits of the air looking on rejoiced, hearing Siddhartha's great pledge. It was the full-moon day of the fourth month, and the sun was about to set.

But the ancient stories tell us that not everyone rejoiced at this moment. There was one force, called Mara, who was terrified and angry. For Mara is the name the Indian people

gave to the evil forces that disturb our minds. Mara is our greed, hatred, ignorance, jealousy, doubt and all the other poisons bringing people unhappiness and grief.

Thus, when Mara saw Siddhartha seated under the Tree of Enlightenment, he was enraged. Calling his sons and daughters around him he shouted, "Look, all of you. Prince Siddhartha is seated in meditation. If he is successful and discovers the way to end all suffering, what will happen to us? Don't you understand that we shall lose all our power? We cannot harm people if he teaches them the truth. We must disturb his meditation, or else we are doomed!"

So Mara and his evil forces tried everything to disturb Siddhartha. They produced a fearful storm and hurled lightning bolts down around him. They churned up a great wind until everything around seemed ready to crash down. But beneath the branches of the tree everything remained calm, protected by the force of Siddhartha's meditation.

Mara saw that the storm had no effect so he turned to his troops and shouted, "Attack!" The whole horde of evil spirits, demons and nightmare shapes turned against Siddhartha. They ran towards him wildly, yelling blood-curdling screams. They shot poisoned arrows of hate at him. But as these arrows flew towards the Prince, they turned into lotus petals and fell harmlessly at his feet. Nothing could disturb the peace of his meditation.

"If these weapons and fearful shapes do not distract him," Mara thought, "perhaps a vision of beauty will disturb his mind." All at once the frightful demons turned into the most beautiful and alluring of women. These bewitching creatures danced in front of the meditator, but even they could not affect him. Memories of the pleasure palaces, visions of his wife and son, heavenly music, delicious food — nothing could break through the calm determination of this seeker of truth.

Mara felt defeated. But he had one last plan. Dismissing his attendants, he appeared alone in front of the Prince. Addressing him in a mocking voice he said, "So you are the great Prince Siddhartha? You think you are a great meditator. So many holy people have failed to find the truth, but you think you will succeed!

"How foolish you are! Don't you know that it takes a great deal of preparation to find the truth you are looking for? What have you ever done to be worthy of success? First you wasted twenty-nine years pampering yourself. Then you wasted six more years starving yourself. Now you sit here thinking that wisdom will just come to you. How foolish! Quit this meditation, or at least show me a witness who will swear that you are worthy of succeeding where all others have failed."

These scornful words failed to bother Siddhartha. Silently he lifted his right hand from his lap, reached in front of him and touched the earth. Yes, the earth itself was Siddhartha's witness! For countless lifetimes he had appeared on this earth in various forms. He had practised generosity and patience, he had acted lovingly and had avoided harming others, and he had meditated on the truth. He had done all these things — sometimes as a man, sometimes as a woman; sometimes rich, sometimes poor — over and over again. He had done all this, just for the sake of discovering the end to all suffering. And the earth was his witness.

Mara realized that now he was truly defeated, and faded away like a bad dream. Siddhartha was left completely alone. The storm clouds parted and the moon shone brightly in the sky. The air smelled sweet and a light dew glistened on the tips of the grass. Everything was ready.

Awakened!

Siddhartha's mind was calm and relaxed. As he sat under the tree his concentration deepened and his wisdom grew brighter. In this clear and peaceful state of mind he began to examine the nature of life. "What is the cause of suffering," he asked himself, "and what is the path to everlasting joy?"

In his mind's eye he looked far beyond his own country, far beyond his own world. Soon the sun, planets, the stars out in space and distant galaxies of the universe all appeared in his meditation. He saw how everything, from the smallest speck of dust to the largest star, was linked together in a constantly changing pattern: growing, decaying and growing again. Everything was related. Nothing happened without a cause and every cause had an effect on everything else.

As he saw how everything was connected in this way, deeper truths appeared to his mind. He looked deeply into himself and discovered that his life as Siddhartha the Prince was but the latest in a series of lifetimes that had no beginning — and he saw that the same was true of everyone. We are born, live and die not one time, but again and again. He saw that death is only the separation of the mind from its present body. After death the mind goes on to find a new body in the same way that a traveller leaves a guest house and moves on to find another. When one life ends, another begins — and in this way the wheel of death and birth keeps spinning around and around.

He also saw that in our travels from one life to the next we are constantly changing and constantly affecting one another. Like actors changing parts in a play, our roles change as we move from life to life. Sometimes we are rich and comfortable; sometimes we are poor and miserable. Occasionally we experience pleasure, but more often we find ourselves with problems. And Siddhartha also saw that as our conditions change, so do our relations with others: we have all been each other's friend and enemy, mother and father, son and daughter thousands upon thousands of times in the past.

Then he looked at all of the suffering in the world. He saw how everyone — from the smallest insect to the greatest king — runs after pleasure, only to end up with dissatisfaction. When we do not find what we are searching for we are miserable, and even when we do find the pleasure we seek it soon fades and we have to look for something else.

And he saw how living beings create their own misery. Blind to the truth that everything is always changing, they lie, steal and even kill to get the things that they want, even though these things can never give them the lasting happiness they desire. And the more their minds fill with greed and hate, the more they harm each other—and themselves! Each harmful action leads them to more and more unhappiness. They are searching for peace yet find nothing but pain.

Finally, he discovered the way to end all this suffering. If a person could see the truth clearly—as he himself had seen it this night—all confused running after pleasure and away from pain would stop. Without any more greed and hatred in our mind, we would never do anything to harm anyone else. Having overcome all the selfishness in our mind, we shall have destroyed the causes of unhappiness completely. With our hatred removed, our hearts will fill with love, and this love will bring us a peace and happiness unlike anything we have ever felt.

When Siddhartha had seen all this, even the last speck of darkness disappeared from his mind. He was filled with a radiant clear light. He was no longer an ordinary person. He had become fully enlightened to the truth. He was now a Buddha, a Fully Awakened One. He had reached his goal!

With a calm and peaceful smile, he arose from his meditation. It was morning, and in the east the sun was beginning to rise.

Whom to Teach?

All of nature rejoiced that glorious morning. Fresh flowers blossomed everywhere and sent their sweet perfume into the air. Birds sang joyfully and creatures everywhere forgot their fear. Rainbows and beautifully coloured clouds appeared in the sky, and people marvelled to see such wondrous sights.

Buddha himself was filled with the highest happiness. His mind, free from all darkness and pain, felt a boundless joy. For days and weeks he stayed near the Tree of Enlightenment, enjoying the bliss and happiness only a buddha knows.

Then he thought, "It was so difficult for me to reach the end of suffering and become a buddha. I had to work so hard for so long. When I see how blind and ignorant most people are, I wonder if there is anyone who can understand the truths I have discovered. How could I possibly teach them? Perhaps it is better for me to live the rest of my life in the forests alone and enjoy the happiness of being a buddha myself."

Then he heard an inner voice which said, "Please do not forget us! We are the suffering beings of the world. We have been waiting for this moment ever since your birth, and even before that. We have hoped and prayed these many years that you would leave the princely life and discover the way to end all suffering. Now that you have found this path, please teach it to us. Unlike you, we are still suffering."

But another thought arose in Buddha's mind: "Who will be able to follow the teachings I have to give? Who is strong and brave enough? Who will try hard and long enough?"

And the inner voice came again: "It is true that our minds are clouded in ignorance, O Buddha. But for some people this ignorance is not so thick. They will be able to understand you. For their sake, please teach us all the true Path!"

Then Buddha smiled and said, "Of course; of course, I shall teach. The only reason I left the princely life was to find a way to help others. Now that I have become a buddha, I shall do everything I can.

"But even a buddha cannot remove the sufferings of others if they do not try to help themselves. People must want to get better before a doctor can cure them. In the same way, they must want to hear the teachings of the truth before anyone can help them. But whoever comes to me with an open mind will find that I am ready to teach them in every way I can."

Then he thought, "Who, among all the people in the world, should be the first I teach? Who is the most ready?" He remembered Arada and Udraka, the two teachers he had met six years before. "They would be the best to teach, but I can see that they have already died and left this world."

Then he thought of the five men who lived with him for so long in the forest. "They are ready to understand the truth," he thought. "I shall teach them first."

He knew that he would find these men in the Deer Park near Varanasi, the holiest city of ancient India. "I shall go there," Buddha proclaimed, "and begin the work I came to do."

The First Teaching

It was a long way to Varanasi and Buddha walked slowly through village and farm. Everyone was immediately attracted to him. He was tall and handsome and moved with dignity and grace. Just seeing him brought calmness and joy to the people. He spoke kind and gentle words of comfort to everyone he met. Whether they were rich or poor, simple or intelligent, of noble birth or low, Buddha treated them all equally, with great love and respect.

Finally, he reached the Deer Park. From a distance the five men saw him approach. Quickly they whispered to one another, "Here comes that good-for-nothing Siddhartha. Let us have nothing to do with such a quitter! Ignore him if he comes near."

But as Buddha approached the men immediately felt that there was something very special about him. Forgetting their plan to ignore him, they automatically stood up as he drew near. With great respect they prepared a seat for him, took his robe, brought him some water and said, "Welcome Siddhartha, to the Deer Park. We are honoured that you have joined us here."

Buddha answered, "I thank you for your kind welcome, O monks. But you should know that I am no longer simply Siddhartha; it is no longer correct for you to call me by that name."

"By what name should we call you then?" they asked.

"The whole world is asleep in ignorance," he answered. "When someone discovers the truth, he or she is asleep no longer. Now I am awake, having discovered the truth. All such awakened ones are called 'Buddha'."

Then the five men, with great respect, said, "O Buddha, please teach us what you have learned so that we too may awaken."

And so, in answer to their request, Buddha delivered his first teaching. It is called "Turning the Wheel of the Dharma" and "Dharma" is the truth he discovered. "O monks," he began, "you must know that there are four Noble Truths. The first is the Noble Truth of Suffering. Life is filled with the miseries of birth, old age, sickness and death. People chase after pleasure but find only pain. Even when they do find something pleasant they soon grow tired of it. Nowhere is there any real satisfaction or peace."

"Second is the Noble Truth of the Cause of Suffering. When our mind is filled with greed or desire, sufferings of all types automatically follow. This ignorant and greedy attitude is the

cause of all our dissatisfaction, robbing us of our peace of mind."

"Third is the Noble Truth of the End of Suffering. When we remove all ignorant craving and desire from our heart, all our suffering and dissatisfaction will come to an end. We shall experience a happiness that is far greater than our ordinary pleasures and a peace that is beyond words."

"Finally, the fourth truth is the Noble Truth of the Path. This path leads to the end of all suffering. If we avoid harming all other living beings, if we sharpen and focus our mind, and if we gain wisdom, each of us can reach perfect happiness, the end of all misery."

When they heard these words the five men felt as happy as if they had found a great treasure of gold. "O Buddha," they said, "you have indeed found the truth. Please teach us the path to perfect wisdom and happiness and we shall be your followers."

It is said that many unseen spirits also heard these first teachings and flew to the ends of the earth crying, "The Buddha has begun to teach. Let all the world rejoice!"

A Mother's Grief

Buddha taught in many ways. To simple people and to children he taught by telling stories. To those of high intelligence he gave detailed explanations of the path. To others he taught without speaking any words at all. But, perhaps, his most powerful teaching was his own example, the very way he lived his life. He always acted with kindness and love. He was patient with everyone, even the most ignorant and foolish.

Very soon, many people were attracted to him and became his followers. If someone had a problem, he or she would go to Buddha and ask his advice. There was one woman, named Gotami, whose child had just died. She was so upset by this that she lost her reason completely. She went everywhere trying to bring her child back to life. Her friends felt sorry for her and said, "Gotami, you should go and see the Buddha. Perhaps he can help you."

She went before Buddha still holding her child in her arms. "Please bring him back to life for me," she cried. Very gently Buddha answered her, "I can help you, Gotami, but first you must bring me something. I need one small mustard seed. However, it must come from a house where no one has ever died."

Gotami quickly went out in search of a mustard seed. She asked at one home and the woman there answered, "Of course you can have a mustard seed. You can have whatever you want —but you should know that last year my husband died."

"Oh," Gotami replied, "then I must search elsewhere," and ran off to the next house.

But wherever she went, the same thing happened. Everyone wanted to help her, but in every family she visited someone had died. One person told her, "Three years ago I lost my daughter." Another said, "My brother died here yesterday." It was always the same.

At the end of the day she returned to the Buddha. "What have you found, Gotami?" he asked. "Where is your mustard seed? And where is your son? You are not carrying him any longer."

She answered, "O Buddha, today I have discovered that I am not the only one who has lost a loved one. Everywhere people have died. I see how foolish I was to think I could have my son back. I have accepted his death, and this afternoon I buried him. Now I have returned to you to hear your teachings. I am ready to listen."

Then Buddha said, "Gotami, you have learned a great deal today. Death must come to everyone sooner or later. But if you learn the truth you can live and die in happiness. Come, I shall teach you." And so he taught her, and soon she found more peace and happiness than she had ever known before.

A Rude Man

Another day Buddha was walking through a village. A very angry and rude young man came up and began insulting him. "You have no right teaching others," he shouted. "You are as stupid as everyone else. You are nothing but a fake."

Buddha was not upset by these insults. Instead, he asked the young man, "Tell me, if you buy a gift for someone, and that person does not take it, to whom does the gift belong?"

The man was surprised to be asked such a strange question and answered, "It would belong to me because I bought the gift."

The Buddha smiled and said, "That is correct. And it is exactly the same with your anger. If you become angry with me and I do not get insulted, then the anger falls back on you. You are then the only one who becomes unhappy, not me. All you have done is hurt yourself.

"If you want to stop hurting yourself, you must get rid of your anger and become loving instead. When you hate others, you yourself become unhappy. But when you love others, everyone is happy."

The young man listened closely to these wise words of the Buddha. "You are right, O Blessed One," he said, "Please teach me the path of love. I wish to become your follower."

And Buddha answered, "Of course. I shall teach anyone who truly wants to learn. Come with me."

Words of Praise

Soon Buddha had a great number of followers, or disciples, who followed him from place to place. One day one of them came up to him and said, "O Blessed One, you are certainly the greatest of all teachers who ever lived!"

Buddha was not flattered by this praise. Instead he asked the disciple, "Tell me, have you met all the great teachers who have appeared in the past?"

"No, of course not," he answered.

"And do you know all the teachers who are alive now or will be born in the future?"

"No, I do not," he answered again.

And so the Buddha said, "Then it is foolish to say that I am the greatest of all teachers. You have no way of knowing if this is true or not."

"But I only wanted to praise you because your teachings are so excellent and helpful," the disciple replied.

Then Buddha said, "If you find my teachings helpful, the best thing to do is practise them. Do not waste your energy praising me. The only reason I have come into the world is to teach others. If you want to please me, follow the teachings. This will please me much more than praise."

At another time Buddha asked a disciple, "If you want to buy some precious gold, will you pay for it without testing it first?"

"No, of course not," was the answer. "It might be fake, and then I would be wasting my money."

"It is exactly the same way with my teachings," Buddha replied. "You should never accept what I say as true simply because I have said it. Rather, you should test the teachings yourself to see if they are true or not. If you find that they *are* true and helpful, then practise them. But do not do so merely out of respect for me.

"Also, do not criticize the teachings of others and say they are no good. There are many other great teachers in the world and they all have their own way of helping people. So do not insult any of them. This is not your business. Your only business is to find happiness and help others find it, too."

In such ways, then, Buddha taught his followers to think for themselves, to be kind to others and to respect everyone.

Kindness to Animals

In those days it was common in India for people to kill animals as a sacrifice, or offering, to their gods. This was supposed to make the gods happy. Then the gods would give the people what they prayed for, such as wealth, or rain for their crops.

Buddha saw that this custom was cruel and mistaken. As he did with the wounded swan when he was still a young boy, Buddha tried to protect the life and relieve the suffering of *all* beings, animal and human alike. He not only wished to save the sheep and cows and other animals from being sacrificed, but he wished to protect the people who wanted to kill these poor animals. He knew that those who sacrificed animals were actually creating the cause for their own future suffering. Buddha taught, "It is not right to make another unhappy so that you can be happy. Everyone wants to remain alive just as you do. Therefore, if you sacrifice an animal, you are just being selfish. And I have said again and again that a selfish person finds nothing but unhappiness in life."

Many of the people who heard these words of wisdom saw that they were true. Immediately they gave up their custom of sacrificing animals. In this way a great deal of unhappiness was brought to an end.

The Power of Love

Buddha never forgot the promise he had made to King Bimbisara to return and give him teachings. So when the time was right, he journeyed to Rajagriha. Outside this royal city was a hill called Vultures Peak, and Buddha and his disciples went and stayed there.

King Bimbisara often went to Vultures Peak to hear the words of Buddha. The people of the city went also, and soon the number of Buddha's followers grew very large. After some time, the King and several other rich people gave Buddha and his followers parks where everyone could stay and listen to his teachings in comfort.

Buddha's cousin, Devadatta, became very jealous. "He has so many people following him," he thought, "and everyone shows him so much respect. I am as great as he is, but they all ignore me. I must destroy him!"

He knew that he would need help in killing the Buddha, so he went to King Bimbisara's son. "Don't you want to be king?" he asked. "Why should your father have all the wealth and power? Come, if you help me kill the Buddha, I shall help you kill your father. Then you can become king in his place."

The King's son listened to these wicked words and agreed. Then the two of them tried many ways to murder the Buddha. One day, while Buddha was sitting in meditation near Vultures Peak, they rolled a very large boulder down the hill towards him. But just before it was going to crush him, the rock split in half, leaving Buddha unharmed.

Another time, Buddha was walking through the city with several of his closest disciples. The two men knew he was coming and were ready. They had bought an elephant and had given it lots of liquor to drink. When it was quite drunk, they beat it with sticks until it was crazed with anger. Then they released it in the direction of the Buddha, hoping the elephant would trample him to death.

When the disciples saw the enraged elephant charging towards them, they ran away in fear. All except Ananda, Buddha's closest companion, who stayed by his teacher's side, holding on to Buddha's robe.

Buddha saw the elephant coming and, instead of being frightened or angry, felt great love and pity for the poor beast. Even though the elephant was drunk and crazed, it felt the power of Buddha's love. It stopped charging, walked over to the Buddha meekly, and bowed down its large head at the awakened one's feet.

Buddha patted the elephant gently and turned and said to Ananda, "The only way to destroy hatred is with love. Hatred cannot be defeated with more hatred. This is a very important lesson to learn."

The Return

One day Buddha said to his followers, "It is time that I returned to Kapilavastu, the city of my father." And so they all began the long walk to Buddha's childhood home. News of Buddha's approach quickly reached the city and everyone became very excited and happy. "At long last our beloved Prince is returning!" they cried. "Now he is a great teacher with hundreds and hundreds of followers. How good it will be to see him again!"

King Shuddhodana was overjoyed to hear of his son's return. When he learned that the Buddha had many followers he became proud and thought, "My son has become a great leader after all. He has brought great honour to my name."

He could not wait for Buddha's arrival, so sent a servant ahead by horse to see what his son was like after so many years. By the next morning the servant had arrived where Buddha and his followers were staying. They were all carrying wooden bowls. They went from door to door in the village begging for their food. Then they returned to where they were staying and ate their simple meal together in silence.

The servant returned to Kapilavastu and reported all of this to the King. The King was furious. He shouted, "My son, a royal prince, has become a beggar! I am disgraced. I must put a stop to this at once!"

Immediately he rode out of the palace and went to where his son was staying. When he saw his Siddhartha, now a radiant buddha surrounded by hundreds of disciples, he was very impressed. They greeted each other lovingly. Then the King asked, "Is it true what I hear, that you beg for your food each morning?"

"Yes," was the answer, "this is true. It is our custom to beg."

At this the King became angrier than he was before. "Our custom?" he shouted. "You come from a long line of kings who never had to beg for anything in their lives. Our custom is to eat from silver and gold plates, not out of simple wooden bowls. What are you talking about, *our* custom?"

The gentle answer came, "Father, you come from a long line of royal kings. This is true. But I come from a long line of teachers, the buddhas of the past. These teachers have always been very humble. They received their food from the people they met. When I say it is our custom to beg, I mean it is the custom of buddhas."

Then he took hold of his father's hands and walked alone with him for a long while. He taught him the Noble Truths and the path leading to the end of all suffering. After listening to him for a long time the King said, "It is true, you are far more than just my son. As the holy man Asita predicted when you were just a baby, you have become a great teacher. I bow before you, O Buddha. Please accept me, who once wanted you to be a king, as one of your disciples."

Soon afterwards Buddha's wife Yasodhara, his son Rahula, the aunt who brought him up and many others from the palace also asked to become his followers. "We were so unhappy when you rode away from us many years ago," they told him. "But now you have brought us so much happiness and peace of mind with your teachings of the truth. We are glad that you left us and have returned as a buddha."

The Tale of the Tree Spirit

From the time he was thirty-five years old, Buddha gave his teachings to everyone who was interested. For the next forty-five years he travelled around India bringing people peace of mind. Sometimes when he wanted to teach people about love and kindness, he would tell them stories that would catch their imagination. Here is one of the stories he told.

A long, long time ago there lived a proud king. He wanted to build a very large palace for himself, so he told his ministers, "Go out into the forest and find the tallest tree there. This I shall use for my palace."

Deep in the forest the ministers found such a tree. It was magnificent and stood surrounded by many other smaller trees. That night they reported back to the King and announced, "Your Majesty, we have found just what you wanted. Tomorrow we shall return to the woods and chop it down."

The King was very happy and went to sleep. That night he had a very strange dream. He dreamt that a spirit, which lived

in that great tree, appeared before him. "O King," it said, "please do not cut down the home in which I live. If you do so, each cut will hurt me very much and I shall die."

But the King answered, "Yours is the finest tree in all the forest. I must use it for my palace."

The spirit pleaded, but the King was very stubborn and insisted the tree would be cut down. Finally the tree spirit said to him, "All right, you may cut it down. But please do it like this. Do not cut it down from the bottom, as people usually do. Instead, have your men climb to the top of the tree and cut it down little by little. First have them cut off one piece, then another, until they have cut down the whole tree."

The King was very surprised by this and said, "But if I have my men do as you say and cut through your tree many times, it will cause you much more pain than if they cut it down just once from the bottom."

The spirit answered, "Yes, this is true. But it is better for the other creatures in the forest if you do as I suggest. You see, my tree is very large. If it falls down in one big piece, it will crash into the other small trees around it and kill many small animals. Many birds and insects will lose their homes and many smaller trees will be destroyed. But if you cut it down piece by piece, it will not do so much damage."

Then the King awoke. He thought, "That spirit would have

let itself be cut a hundred times so that the small animals of the forest would not suffer. How brave and kind it is! And how selfish of me to want to cut that tree down for my own pleasure and pride. Instead of cutting it down, I should honour it! This dream has taught me that I should also be kind and gentle to everyone."

And so the King went into the forest the next day and decorated the tree. And he was a kind and just ruler from that day onwards.

Equal Love to All

One day Devadatta fell ill. Many doctors came to see him but no one could cure him. Then his cousin, the Buddha, went to visit him.

One of Buddha's followers asked him, "O Buddha, why are you going to help Devadatta? He has tried to harm you many times. He has even tried to kill you!"

And Buddha answered, "There is no reason to be friendly with some people and an enemy to others. All people are equal in that everyone wants happiness and no one likes to be sick and miserable. Therefore, we should have love for everyone."

Then he approached Devadatta's bed and said, "If it is true that I love Devadatta, who is always trying to harm me, as much as I love Rahula, my only child, then let my cousin be cured of his sickness!" Immediately Devadatta recovered and was healthy once again.

Buddha turned to his followers and said, "Remember, we should not be kind to some and cruel to others, but instead should try to cultivate equal love for all. This is the way of the enlightened ones."

The Final Days

When Buddha was eighty years old he thought to himself, "I have done all I could to help others. I have taught them how to live with love and how not to fear anything in life. Now it is time to show them how to leave this world without fear."

So he called the faithful Ananda to him and said, "Ananda, it is time for us to return to Kapilavastu for the last time. I wish to die in the city where I grew up."

Ananda was grief stricken. "O Buddha," he cried, "please do not leave us! For so many years you have been our guide. What shall we do without you?" Then he began to sob bitterly.

Buddha answered, "Do not cry, dear Ananda. I have always taught that death is a natural part of life. It is nothing to fear. You must understand that. And when I am gone, let my teachings be your guide. If you have understood them in your heart, you have no more need of me. Come, let us go."

And so Buddha and his disciples travelled north. Not far from Kapilavastu they passed through the village of Kushinagar. The Buddha asked them to stop there and rest. Then he turned to Ananda and said, "This is where I shall pass away."

Although this was to be the last day of his life, Buddha did not stop helping others. An old man from the village asked to see him, and Buddha agreed. He listened to the man's problems and gave him kind words of advice. The man was put at ease and felt happy once again.

Then Buddha went out into the garden and lay down between two trees. His followers gathered around him. Some were crying, but others, their minds completely at peace, looked on silently.

Then Buddha spoke for the last time. "Remember what I have taught you. Craving and desire are the cause of all unhappiness. Everything sooner or later must change, so do not become attached to anything. Instead devote yourself to clearing your mind and finding true, lasting happiness."

Buddha then turned onto his right side and placed his right hand under his head. He closed his eyes and very peacefully passed away. It was the full moon day of the fourth month.

After some time, his disciples took his body and placed it on a large pile of wood. They were going to burn it, as was the custom, but they could not get the fire to start. Then Buddha's main disciple arrived. He had been away when Buddha died, and hurried to Kushinagar as soon as he found out about Buddha's passing. After he arrived and paid his last respects to his teacher, the wood caught fire by itself. It burned for a long time, until nothing was left but some ashes and a few bones.

The different kings who lived in north India at that time all wanted the ashes and bones of the Buddha. They thought, "I shall build a monument to this great teacher in my kingdom, and place his remains inside it. This will bring me and my kingdom great honour."

Since each of the kings wanted the remains, they soon began to quarrel. "They are mine," said one. "No, they belong to me," said another. Finally, a wise person said, "Buddha spent his entire life teaching us how to love one another. Now, after he has passed away, you foolish people are about to fight over his ashes. Fighting is against everything he ever taught us. So instead, let us divide up his remains equally. Then each of you can build a separate monument to him in your own kingdom."

The kings realized the wisdom of these words, and stopped their quarrelling. They divided the ashes and bones of the Teacher among themselves and returned to their kingdoms. There they built monuments to the memory of one who taught and lived the path of peace and wisdom.

The Teachings Still Live

The story of Buddha took place 2500 years ago, but it still has not come to an end. Just as Buddha came to this earth to show us all the path to enlightenment, even now the awakened ones are showing this same path to countless others in far-away worlds. In those lands they take birth, search for the truth, show the way to awaken from ignorance and then pass away, all for the sake of leading others to happiness.

And the buddhas have not abandoned those of us on this planet. Although we cannot see them with our eyes, it is still possible to find them with our heart. For all of us have the pure buddha-nature within, and the more we overcome our closed-minded selfishness, the more we open ourselves to the rays of inspiration that shine continuously from all the buddhas in the universe.

Although Buddha passed away a long time ago in a small village in India, his teachings of love and wisdom have never died. His disciples who lived with him first mastered and then passed on his teachings to others. And they in turn taught them to still others. In this way they have reached us today.

142

Everyone, in every country, no matter what he or she believes, can learn from these teachings of the compassionate Buddha. By following them properly, we can get rid of all selfishness, hatred and greed. We can conquer all fear and reach the same peace and understanding that Prince Siddhartha found under the Tree of Enlightenment. In the same way that he did, we can each become a buddha, an awakened one. We can bring the same happiness to others that he did.

May all beings be happy!

Not to commit any harm,
To do good,
And to purify one's mind:
This is the teaching of the awakened ones.